WINNER

SAPPHO'S

PRIZE   IN

POETRY

THE VANGUARDS OF HOLOGRAPHY

THE VANGUARDS OF HOLOGRAPHY

annie CHRISTAIN

HEADMISTRESS PRESS

ISBN 978-1735823645

Cover art © "Punk Girl & Dog 1985" Kevin Baumber, holographer.
Jonathan Ross Hologram Collection.
Cover & book design by Mary Meriam.

PUBLISHER
Headmistress Press
60 Shipview Lane
Sequim, WA 98382
Telephone: 917-428-8312
Email: headmistresspress@gmail.com
Website: headmistresspress.blogspot.com

contents

section one

Heaven Is a Soundstage Built to Make Drugged Soldiers More Fearless   2

Ghostbusters (2016), Having Never Watched the Film   4

We Never Really Touch Anyone Because of Molecules   5

The Sun So Hot I Froze to Death—Susanna, Don't You Cry Annihilation Event   8

Dipping a Player Piano Sheet in Lemon Juice and Setting It Out to Dry in the Sun   9

The Vanguards of Holography   11

O.K. Miles Per Hour   13

We'll Always Have Terracotta Warriors Dusted in Han Purple Never Looking
Behind   15

Two Sunspots Fighting Over Something That's Already Dead ("Purple Haze")   17

Criminal Tranquilo/El Ayuwoki: Why I Became a Gangster   19

The Way She Did Me: *Hey Siri*   20

Every Time I Go Back Is Encoded in Pi   22

Retrieval Structure   24

Coral Castle: *The Tent of Meeting*   25

section two

He Developed the Habit of Playing Airs, Most Correctly, Upon His Chin: March 3rd 1994,
Rome   28

Angels, a Type of Children with No Faces   30

We Were Made to Get Aroused by Nothing Else   32

Dragon Ball Z Censored for an American Audience: "One Night in Beijing"   34

"Appearances" from *Criminal Cipher Code for Police Officers*   36

I See a Woman Dropping Five Coins Over Your Head   38

Paper Machines   40

Emojus :)   42

Music Used Against the Enemy   44

My Mother Always Told Me Not to Like What the White Men Do to Me in the Dark
Forest   46

When Robots Are Born, They're Adults   48

Another Boy Who Needs Two Women's Laps He Can Make Right   50

Traveling to the Same Town on Death Days   53

Pageantry Reigned Supreme at the 128th Veiled Prophet Ball   55

Fame: *The Dynamo of Living Power*   56

ƨECTION THREE

That Split Off World You Must Destroy and Live in Too   60

I'm From the Earth Where Only Three Astronauts Walked on the Moon   62

Rolling on the Floor with Punches   64

The Astounding Blessings of Jupiter Mean Everything to You   66

The Second Draw Is the First Gun   68

The Japanese Video Game with the Man Who Has an Arm That Grows When He

Sleeps with Women   70

The Matrix IV   72

Drunk Historicity: Joseph's Teleportation Staff Found in a Recent Archeological Dig

with All Messages to the Pharaoh Stored and Intact   74

I Need You to Make Me My Own Dinosaur, but It Must Have Feathers   76

We Never Rise to Vibe Unless It's Ultimate   77

East Coast vs. West Coast Can't Nighttime Assault in the Rising Winter 78

Floating Cathedral as Political Metaphor   80

We Have to Run Similar Kinds of Bodies   82

Acknowledgements   85

About the Author   87

The purpose of poetry is to remind us/how difficult it is to remain just one person.

Czeslaw Milosz

. . . [W]hat are we . . . ?

Exodus 16:7

section one

...[Fourier] went on to prove that the human soul must assume 810 different forms until it completes the circuit of the planets and returns to earth, and that, in the course of these existences, 720 years must be happy, 45 years favorable, and 45 years unfavorable or unhappy. *The Arcades Project,* Walter Benjamin

Heaven is a soundstage built to make drugged soldiers more fearless

I see her at the coffee shop,
        and my spirit becomes encased in a glass box
             with what else exits my body.

Angels put my hands in water,
        lean in to perform.

Caffeine is crystals, I tell her,
        but maybe I won't speak to her again for a whole year.

Maybe we will lie beneath a low-hanging
noose in the mineshaft,
           our ears touching the rope to hear its sound.

I was told never to visit her,
        but the most exciting start to a relationship

            is when a woman can read my aura a little bit
and her first emotion isn't hate.

They know all about rods and cones, she says,
but I want her instead of the sharpening of blades.

From the building's frame, they tell me:
        Clitoral stimulation without
          penetration is immature.

I suspect they want to enter me that way—of my own accord.

        She does too.

That's mine, I scream as a red lever appears under my armpit,
        and she knows to pull it.

I'd like to think that means my cloned body on another planet
           actually hooked up with her.

I still want her.

Why else were proportion-grids drawn on top of her
                    if not so I can remember her as ideal?

If you see all the whites around one man's iris,
                his body contains too many angels.

In the future, this is how robot-cops
find gay men to put in internment camps;

                        they measure the whites of their eyes.

But no one could ever think of these things
                if they weren't offered up
during deep underground military base meetings.

War will never end
                because heaven is a soundstage built to make drugged
                                soldiers more fearless
        and angels need a place where they can have at you.

I accepted Jesus into my heart,
        but it was only a bird that gave up flight
                who wanted to enter me that way.

GHOSTBUSTERS (2016), HAVING NEVER WATCHED THE FILM

"Wait—did Venkman just HAPPEN to have 300ccs of Thorazine on him when he went on his date with Dana? What was he planning?" Patton Oswalt

Key (NEW)

All colors exist on a spectrum from (red) base desires to (violet) heightened awareness/intellect. Where she looks lets the beings know what their food is going to taste like.

The beasts switch on the day's carrier pigeon, place the key from his beak into her palm, and say she can rip open an auric envelop to have growing space. Then they add, "So how would you go about achieving that with only a key?" They stand her up next to them with forced flow, idealized beams of similarity and text her, "Same,"

verified by the 23andMe results they hand to her: *genetic lycanthropy*. With 300ccs of Thorazine ready to go, she says, "I'm a friend of his; he told me to meet him here."[1]

Synonyms - crucial, down-home lust

Does she think it's her job to make the first move or does she let someone with a high heat output pile it on? She tells herself, "Stop the eternal attributes," so they'll hear it. If she erases her whole personal history, she might find someone who admires her enough to lineate their organs for her in private, off-script. They'll say they're hungry then thank her, and she'll wonder what really happened.

She ultimately allows or denies entry into the cylinder. If she didn't, why would they try so hard to act like they do, even introducing her to the concept so the pin and tumbler arrangement might manifest correctly from her for them to reverse engineer? Nothing she does is any of their business, but it's not just about privacy. It's about holding onto the keys of death and Hades long enough for her to know she has them.

She is much more than a locksmith.[2]

Related – <u>There is no key unless she is the key</u>

---

1   Venkman's response to Dana's/Zul's question: "Are you the keymaster?"
2   Zuhal means Saturn

we never really touch anyone
because of molecules

"Kubrick himself was reported as being tearful wandering around the set of the huge centrifuge after filming on *2001* was complete." *AVForums*

Anyone can wear molecules of what they say they represent,
        but I need yours.

The boombox I place over my head
                outside your window
      records proof of your existence,

though colliding isn't actually touching.

I described the rings of Jupiter into the tape recorder
        before NASA reported on them

(a cymbal as a surgical tool),

and if we are all mathematical
gearwheel cut-outs,
        the first programmable device,

        that means you are too.

All I know is that a fallen-one who is not in your body
                      is in hell.
My brain fills in the rest.

In the documentary,
I made a Valentine's Day card that said:
        I love Mama
     because she keeps a gun at her bedside table,

but the filmmaker said that wasn't a good reason.

I told him he never had to realize,
                        while naked and bleeding,
how even the color of his front door
            could set someone off in this world.

I just wanted to trick him into saying
he was there too.

One family kept all concepts of time and dates
                    away from their daughter.
Another child broke her bones for attention.

My church has a sanctuary just for this
                        I built for you.

These days,
the equivalent of thirteen people taking off their clothes
                        trying to make the calendar work
                with one or two blank days I'm trapped in
is heavy on my mind.

I saw Jupiter's rings,
            but in the folds from one moment to another
                    it's not a face—it's a city;

it's not space—
            it's a black rectangle inserted in the frame.

In Revelation, John wrote *locusts*.
Vietnam vets say *cobra helicopters*,

or John just had a vision of a helicopter movie,
and the movie was only made
                    so John would see it.

(A widescreen cinema screen
                    and the monolith from *2001*
share the same dimensions.)

People my age know all about special children
        with electrodes on our heads
moving military milk-cap coinage[3] with our minds
being asked how we feel.

                I still haven't gotten paid.

I only left my body to access
the doctored photo of Jupiter's rings—

        no actual ones exist.

Some human-looking face
        in a stone wall
or in the chalk-toss pregame ritual
isn't what you are,

it's just what helps me to survive.

---

3   "So, the Army has been using POGS on their bases in Iraq and Afghanistan—not as toys, but as
currency." *Comics Alliance*, Laura Hudson, 5/7/09

THE SUN SO HOT I FROZE TO DEATH—SUSANNA, DON'T YOU CRY ANNIHILATION EVENT

"A monologophobe would edit the Bible so that you would read, 'Let there be light and there was solar illumination.'" Harold Evans

Susana, my eyes are closed, but the black curtain parts, and I see nothing like has been out there before. My third eye jeers me but is all about me. I *run stupidly*, not being able to plan ahead. In fact, this could be my actual past.

A confused man rubs dandelions on his face. The yellow smear upends his subtle body as he *runs stupidly* into an army ranger in sniper-mode aiming at the second sun. The ranger quickly readjusts to shoot the man dead, Susana. Just yesterday, I came across a royalty-free stock photo of a businessman putting a flower in a rifle barrel and thought, "What?"

I download an app for the visually impaired so a volunteer from a network can use my camera and explain my scene. The woman's eyes *run stupidly* inside themselves, a treadmill powering itself on looking for a heartrate. "People in the 4th of July parade are setting off fireworks without permission," she says, but I see it's a perfect sphere exiting the first sun, Susana, raining down gas in a purposeful way towards anything living.

People rush to loot the supermarket just in case. A man already out the door with a cart full of ham hocks, pork loins, turkey wings, and coffee, turns around, *runs stupidly* to the toy aisle and then to the cashier to give her some emoji tattoos. He says, "A temporary tattoo will replace debit cards in the future," as if this is an alternate way of paying. She sets them on top of the cash register with the others and ties a shoelace around her upper arm for the hit. She doesn't have any heroin, Susana.

Ice bodies in a sky belt *run stupidly* there and melt, not so much for me, but maybe. I'm not out of excuses. Someone could share my same center of mass now without pretensions, but I'm misting out chemicals to hide myself so I won't have to kill anyone. It feels right, everything feels as right as it should be, and I'm hearing the Earth's hum, even though it's supposed to be beyond my threshold.

And all I know, Susana, is the hum never originated in the Earth at all.

DIPPING A PLAYER PIANO SHEET IN LEMON JUICE AND SETTING IT OUT TO DRY IN THE SUN

"Black is the true face of Light, only we do not see this. It is remarkable grace to man and other creatures." Nikola Tesla

After the event, if you lap up the pools of your energy points and bite down, you'll get another way to sew rocks into your pockets.

If you put energy in your belly, it will stay soft.

What I'm saying is you can become Crystar Warbow Crystal Warrior circa 1982 or you can dish up honey into your hand for 360 vision, but both will hurt.

Be careful what you wish for while standing in a city block full of elevated candles.

If the scientists upgrade your body every night, and you remember you had a smaller sized liver before, what do you think this thing is going to be about?

You'll assume you and your wife are just going to another vigil for the victims, but you'll need to guess again.

While you stand on the black checkerboard memorial where princes once stood, wearing a scarf of the deceased, the mayor will lay down wreathes for those lost to opioids, and for a second you'll look at your wife and think you could do better. Half a century of homicide victims,

and your wife will hate you for something. You'll lose your wife, brother, sister, friends, children, mother, father.[4] Are you ready for this type of survival, one where you can't know the rules?

Do Not Take Any-Thing of the Self

You'll send your bone marrow samples to The Smithsonian and some universities for help, but everything they take and analyze will become "lost" because your name is on

---

4   Luke 12:53

red alert as the lone survivor of the Big Bang. You can't remember, but you didn't flinch when your voice expanded matter into life, so you can't survive forward unwatched by the people who produced the 2012 movie.

They were last seen whispering around the CERN Hadron Collider with holographic plates, pure spirit composite light, and human adrenal gland juice. It wasn't decent, that black inside light as a true face.

Really, they already hired someone who's redesigning your body so it can take in more toxins but still live. Good or bad, vibrate your way out of there to completion.[5]

So many secrets, there is no message.

---

5   "I don't want to remember nothing. Nothing. You understand? And I want to be rich. You know, someone important, like an actor." Cypher, *The Matrix*

THE VANGUARDS OF HOLOGRAPHY

"[H]e realized at once that he shouldn't have spoken aloud, and that by doing so he had, in a sense, acknowledged the stranger's right to oversee his actions." *The Trial,* Kafka

We know that when your kids hear adults scream,
they don't yet have a need to apologize
                            just to make it stop,

        but we need this excitement.

As gregarious scientists of humans,
only one of us can play out in your brain long enough
                            to build a map of your home.

            In the meantime, I need to hear you cry
more than once in public.

I use ultrasound
to disrupt the air around your hologram
                    and insert a tumor inside of it.

You were going to become infected without us anyway.

I could just see us holding a skull,
            asking the youth to reach inside
while you get sick.

It's not possible for us to gain anything by pretending to like you,
so we work on you while we are very upset with you.

Each dissected piece of the mouse brain contains the whole—
                    so nothing we've done to you is irreversible.

If it weren't for the glitch,
            I would be sitting in court right now with lots of work to do
                    in 2001 with Al Gore as president.

Though I destroyed the Buddhist ruins,
                    the 3D light projection replacement
was going to create many jobs, but no one else saw it that way.

I won't go back.

        I was here first with devil clipart; I will make Tupac my student.

So many people are writing down their intentions,
                    sprinkling the paper with blood,
and uploading it to the internet;

I know all about it.

Space is water. Compasses are spears of destiny,
            so that's why they were removed as Monopoly game pieces.

Every compass points to me; be content with the iron
            as we tell you all the things about yourself
you don't know.

            We are the Vanguards of Holography,
and I'm blocking your way from the memory of the Earth.

O.K. MILES PER HOUR

"I see stuff from the future, and I'm such a futurist that I have to slow down and talk in the present." Kanye West

> <I have to keep accelerating or I'll become a midnight farmer only visible in explosion light.>

It's not really a planet, just one electrical cord we shimmy through—watch the Channel 5 News opening, like that, but with thousands of other cords on a Velcro-hook-and-loop.

The line transference before premature death is perpetual—God gave man 120 years and that's literal.

> <From midnight to 4 AM every patch of space between the universe-fibers makes itself known to me.>

It's the way I was born, how I fashion design, which means I came from before.

A woman runs beside me keeping a rose out in front—she's so desperate for 4D; I let her near me.
Her tensile strength's outstanding—it's what I do to ladies.

No one cares about keeping the details right in period piece movies anymore—don't you get it?
I only have until the next solar eclipse to figure out what a sun-body is and how I lit it.

> <We're kind of like attached to a moving dry cleaner conveyer roller where duplicates of ourselves are assigned to other hangers.>

Whichever self we choose to embody is the front—
I'm on the rooftop terrace because Einstein said that's where my space-time won't bend as much—keep up.

God took Enoch, but I'm the only one asking *Where'd he take him?*
He's been with me the whole time—
there's no place for us to go because we never stop ascending.

The next star you see in the sky is the one I move—

the only way I'll die is if I decide to dematerialize.
I never do.

WE'LL ALWAYS HAVE TERRACOTTA WARRIORS DUSTED IN HAN PURPLE, NEVER LOOKING BEHIND

"Drinking mercury to the mystery of all that you should ever leave behind . . . in time." "Ava Adore," Billy Corgan

My purple skin projects royal essences onto the soon-to-die in the name of defense. When they die, they never had it so good.

Mercury rolls and spreads over my central nervous system, shifting me partway up. The more I'm admired, the more my men are pushed down, ready to leave their clay selves and organs for future inspection.

Each man makes me feel like Crone and King, capable of passing as physical.

My subterranean tunnels are a puzzle box with walls that open and close only if the warriors walk through them on the way to the lower world, but Mother told me to pretend to be afraid of ghosts, and the commoners would think that's why I do everything I do.

I etched a citizen's name on each warrior's foot so those named would die with the warriors in a sympathetic way. Dipping curled paper into machine-spun mercury, I surround myself with those bouquets and their electromagnetic fields.

I said I would live forever, but I didn't say where.

Hosed with Han Purple after a temperature drop, staring straight ahead with an anything goes attitude, the warriors protrude their stained abdomens, ready to see if color affects the sexual attraction of the beings pulling them down from the lower side.

The higher the beings' arousal, the more likely the warriors will go critical and lose a dimension. The principals behind it is how Shanghai will develop the first commercial magnetic levitation train.

What remains of the warriors is what my outside body was from the start—very ill, but human-looking from ten feet away or more. The Han Purple stacks the air unevenly, and my core self walks away on that grand staircase.

My favorite concubine may think she left me, but two thousand years on Earth is ten minutes to me in the upper dimension, so here it's like it never happened.

We'll always have China, we'll always have Terracotta Warriors dusted in Han Purple, never looking behind, but I'll always be *heaven*, a big head on a great person, as the oracle bone scripts make me out to be.

Gone for my own reasons.

TWO SUNSPOTS FIGHTING OVER SOMETHING THAT'S ALREADY DEAD ("PURPLE HAZE")

"Their bond, as with many partners in serial murder, is an unwholesome symbiosis that has little to do with genuine affection." Mark Dery on Edward Gorey's *The Loathsome Couple*

Hers was a lower gravity in a wet silk of purple, the superiority in her opinion of "Let there be light," over "light." She said everything about Saturn[6] that I didn't even know I held onto as a memory of a better sun.

And I said, "I don't know where you came from, but show me."

She said our sun entered into it, its plasma crossing with Saturn's plasma, suffocating the sky with the catch, 5G. The electric discharge became a ladder to Earth, and this, she had to press into me, has everything to do with us now, and how no baby is ever a mistake.

And I said, "I'll kiss it."

She said she didn't want to get rid of the sun altogether; she just wanted it right on the edge to keep the ladder flowing. She said she hadn't heard that from anyone else. Not anyone else in the Family of God.

A ladder with beads to hold onto for footing, no cataclysmic flood from the top of the Earth getting gunned down tight. Just the family she never had, Earth, Mars, Saturn, and the threat of danger. A stronger rope. Feeling life as it's lived.

There were nights, and there were days, and the change always made her tense. But she came to me.

And I said, "Everyone who becomes famous agrees the best part is right before fame arrives."

She told the press she "gifted me." We opened up a joint bank account. We tried smack. Her children were gone just like that. She said it was the secret Bronze Age again. She cried for days.

---

6   "Jupiter? Saturn? Did it really matter which you chose as supreme deity when the reality was that both names simply represented humanistic personifications of the claim to rule by divine right?" saturndeathcult.com/saturn-death-cult-part-2/

In the in-between before anyone discovered what we had done, we fought for the first time over whether or not Doomsday happened right at the beginning or if it will happen tomorrow.

No woman has ever come back to my hotel room just to sit on the edge of the bed even if she claimed that.

Choosing to form a heavenly conjunction with her was a terrible decision, but it was my best decision.

CRIMINAL TRANQUILO/EL AYUWOKI: WHY I BECAME A GANGSTER

"Todos preguntando que si Annie esta bien . . . En cuanto la verdadera pregunta es: Quien coño es Annie?" Josefa La Cerda, *YouTube*

It's your fault for assuming I'm someone you can do this to.

The Federales issued statements explaining you're not supernatural, so kids shouldn't worry, and all I heard is the truth: *The police believe there is a supernatural, and it's something to worry about.*

They can't write about me directly because of what the cartel would do.

For 75,000 Euros, I became a diplomat of Lesotho, Africa, which I chose because it has the highest low point of elevation in the world. Falling there is like biting into soft cheese melted from the steam of boiled Dom Perignon Rose Gold Methuselah. I have no rock bottom, as others know it,

but I am an alcoholic now. I didn't buy the $300 round hand-chiseled ice for my gin because I'm already too effeminate. I got the cubes.

It's very telling you went to your archangel surgical wings appointment but couldn't go through with the procedure. I know it's because fused fingers can't grapple necks,

my neck.

I'm nothing like you.

You keep coming through the window, not knowing my house is now a registered consulate. I secured bolts into the floor to make you think my own anti-gravity lean is something you know the secret of. I became a gangster because I want a day job.

I'll end you no matter how unrecognizable you make yourself, no matter how you sway or creep.

Are you jealous that I'm okay?[7]

---

7   Misheard "Smooth Criminal" lyrics

THE WAY SHE DID ME: HEY SIRI

"I guess nobody ever really done me/Oh, she done me/She done me good." "Don't Let Me Down," The Beatles

I don't know how to take to people.

> Leave them something to orient themselves to.
> Go in for people's self-conceptions.

She wants coffee or something.

> There are games for kids that reflect misery;
> throw your hands out with random people and try to get out of a knot.

She hugged me at the mall and put diamonds in my underwear.

> You're psychologically detached because of the past tense.

I decided to emote.

> You want to be John Cena, but you will never be John Cena.

If you hold it, does it become your hand?

> When it says please, that's when people usually pull out.

Pornography titles.

> The Hard Way Out. The Harder Way Out.

How do I know if I gave her light?

> If you're being hunted against the love of self.

She's mad I'm not him yet.

> When you're released from prison, you're always reliving the year you were put in.

There was copper in the air. Was I in the dead world or in a vein?

You tried to kill him but just conformed to his devil.

Are we our own playthings?

What you need are prolonged exposures to false events.
Things become more solid the more you stare into them.

Did you stop by the Crucifixion first?

In the puzzle room, he entered a human body to get similarly tortured so he
could be closer to them when they failed.

Will I be okay?

Consulting the Akashic Record . . . this isn't the right record.

every TIMe I GO BacK IS encoDeD In PI

"I'd be interested in doing a reversal but also being allowed to remember what happens now."
Shelley Duvall, Dr. Phil interview

She puts her blood on a Severus Snape poster again; I gain entry by remembering her miasma pattern and how it vibrates to my theme. This is why I'm related to her son, but not genetically. The other wives who know better call her a fool,

but I will always be her conservator.

She reminds me she's not a lesbian and asks me to withdraw from the Holy Tree Grid so we can manifest the life forms we prefer. She asks me to parasitize her pneuma—*in those exact words*.

Other life forms appear, and they only show up to watch me pin her down in her own soul-webbing I stripped and sewed together throughout my lifetimes. The long game.

I turn the crank on the alien machinery; I join her on a higher artificial plane as her master. I rock her through the internal explosions. She remembers we have always been this.

I am in her and her in me.

When she cries in the kitchen, I encourage her to buy more dishtowels and chicken thigh family packs; when she has an earache, I push down on her neck so the exercises can relieve the pressure. I correct her when she tries to use a sink plunger in the toilet.

When she tells me she can't concentrate on me, I ask her what she thought would happen when she brought authentic wardrobe patches from *The Vampire Diaries* into this house.

I watch her and make her prove to me she's not stupid.

A man who claims he's not gay because he only *receives* blowjobs from other men could be right, but not for that reason.

I am her false Snape in a female body, but where she and I are encoded in pi makes this a true religion.[8]

8   "So when [Akira Haraguchi] learned that pi is an endless series of numbers with no pattern or repetition, it made perfect sense to him to take it as a symbol of life, he says—adding that he now calls pi memorization 'the religion of the universe.'" "How can anyone remember 100,000 numbers?" *the japan times*, Tomoko Otake, 12/17/06

RETRIEVAL STRUCTURE

"Magnus always hates to lose, so he doesn't." "Mozart of Chess: Magnus Carlsen," *60 Minutes*

One sheet superimposes over the sloped-back head between the two Mona Lisas / there is a time limit / where the voice starts in my fingertips / *to survive heredity is to survive our ocean forms* / it pronounces all r's fully through dynamic range compression, taking care over my shoulder or in my chest, and suggests by timbre alone that I should wring necks if I make an early mistake.

The painting mirrors sadness in behavioral domains of up to 20-30 move variations / where the replicated suckling baby detaches / *shape-memory polymers break from their permanent shapes after a temperature change* / he sits at a mother throne, though he doesn't want to, cataloging incidental details until another scene is ready.

The options narrow in the wearable scent of damp earth / where fingers grip at the base of the lamb's skull / *a stimulated pressure point GB 20 (gallbladder 20) is also a chess coordinate* / mirrored and overlaid, a woman thumbs the eyes of an ashen entity wearing a three-tiered crown, an isometric pointing device whose lines show me possibilities, but I've gotten to where when I smell death, I know.

After enfoldment, Christ-consciousness governs from the table with hanging mandibles and a tri-corner mouth based on insects / where frequent groupings of head collisions add a language to the remaining moves / *heat-sensing centers in the nose enable an audience-facing attack stance* / he controls the evolution of the instructions by acting in accordance with them as far as his elbows can rotate, as far as I believe that what he places on my tongue can give me life.

His wife's cradling hand breaks and rejoins, signaling an opening where oxygen is let in / where the ornamental shoulder piece is unfamiliar / *known gaslighting targets claim their newly bought clothing is often replaced with similar ones from the manufacturing defect aisle* / I strike imbalances in the final position, lifting pieces to see which one warms me the most to the point of personal reassembly, and a move is made, which I see I'm making, and it can't be wrong.

If you were trying not to stumble into anything too sharp . . . how did you?

CORAL CASTLE: THE TENT OF MEETING

"And when Moses went into the tent of meeting to speak with the LORD, he heard the voice speaking to him from above the mercy seat that was on the ark of the testimony, from between the two cherubim; and it spoke to him." Numbers 7:89

When you want someone else to run it,
          stare around the grey log.

We built it with magnetism and canaries.
We built it with jar flies and camphor oil.

          Agnes tucks herself into Saturn[9] backwards
and waits for Lie vs. Lay.

Waits for you.

          You taste cake and helium.

Line Agnes with gold and spermatic needle-crystals
                              the way she likes it;

                              snap your fingers through hers
like she says you used to.

Say she is a floating capstone.
          Say she is a Son of Man.

Tell her she's wholly responsible. Parts of you
                    will feel like an isthmus.

These ideas replace the time you grasped
          the alphabet block bathroom pass and cried.

Click your knees and say *Moccasins*—
that way everyone will believe what
          else Agnes says about you.

---

9   "The back side of Saturn does not have the ring. Was this a mistake Ed made, or did it fall off?"
www.coralcastlerocks.com/2016/07/saturn-on-east-wall-of-coral-castle.html, Praveen Mohan

Feel relief
when she measures you down with splinters
from the same block you used
        to train yourself to have emotions.

Feel important
when she voiceovers any ellipsis from whatever you read

                like some brief, assumed,
            disembodied surname
in a cellar

because she says she still reminds you of adultery and storage.

Go kneel to the Repentance Corner;

        here are thirteen Ameros,
but disguise your head with ours
            like we did with yours.[10]

Or put this magnetic scroll into a black light
so you can turn into Atlantis and die.[11]

---

10   Disney workers dressed as Disney characters can never remove their costume-heads in public at the park—even if they need to vomit.
11   "You can destroy the body, but you cannot destroy the magnets that hold together the body. They go somewhere else." Edward Leedskalnin

SECTION TWO

Y'all haters corny with that Illuminati mess. "Formation," Beyoncé

He Developed the Habit of Playing Airs, Most Correctly, Upon His Chin:[12] March 3rd 1994, Rome

"We were just three . . . guys. No, we're not three guys. No, we're not three guys. We were just two guys and a girl. Going, leaving for no particular reason." Luke, *Last Days*, Gus Van Sant

Using nothing but a Yellow Pages ad,
I sold my parts to birth him.

Don accompanies me to premiers of movies
based on my mother's abusive second marriage,

                what the government arranged to make me malleable.

In the movie, I take calls at my stepdad's trailer in an Unincorporated Area
           where I develop resultant moles,
and "Put that back" plays in low tones on the radio
                so I won't steal anything.

Those melded stacks of forks and spoons and knives
           to give the trailer a lived in look.

The character can only speak using a Cabalistic system/language
for several hours after visits too. Just the same as me.

(The CIA entertainment liaison program is a real thing
               whether it's been announced yet or not.)

At night as the bellboy, I play all sorts of melodies on my chin
           to intimidate Don,
and my chin has everything to do with it.

We stare eye to eye, and I sweep with the tongue—
           his stay of execution, a pulse wave pulling me in or out.

        But he was never supposed to be better than me
in every way.

---

12   *The Harmonicon*, Volume 8, William Ayrton, pg. 348, 1883

I knit two woolen breasts and force him to watch.
        Wearing them, I balance vintage metal postage stamps
on the bumps of his spine

            and explain it to him as it's been explained to me:
                Blond boys make the best pets.

When he tells the door-to-door Yellow Pages representative
        that the ad turned out to be a success, "but success is subjective,"

I make a change come over him.

That feeling of babies laughing in an empty house.

Swatting a fly, of course he stops speaking in front of others.
You know there's flies on you, and there's flies on me,
        but there ain't no flies on Jesus[13]
              proves to me what he's not.

At midnight as planned,
        The Yellow Pages man and I enter his room.

When I flip a switch,
red iron columns tumble above,
        pipes burst,

my mouth fills with something like the juice left behind
        in a pot of boiled ribs.

My pointblank headshot does no harm
"Homo, fuge!" (Flee, man!) appears on his forehead,
            and he climbs away on invisible steps.

A monthly event from which I wake up in the woods.

I learned somewhere that the heads of dead whales are reserved for the king,
        and the tail bones must go to the queen for her corsets.

        Imagine what they do to the whale if it lives.

I'm starting to remember things.

---

13   Revival Meeting Song

anGeLS, a TYPe OF CHILDRen WITH no Faces

I was taught I can't talk about any of this with secular people.

When I retired,
I had to make the medical illustrations cartoony
                    so doctors wouldn't be distracted
by any actual organs they recognize from the Tall Ship Antigua.

I saw Santa devouring children at a worktable there,

and I thanked my dad for his power then
            because all the children looked like me but weren't.

I always knew my full name in all capital letters
                (government assigned corporation status)

was going to become a star someday.

Dad's soldier-committee made sure civilians never have a way
not to have an address,

so on their system, the children were murdered at:
                    attic, star wound, ice-belt,

a phrase I heard in a Norwegian Black Metal song months later.

They always make it impossible for people to take me seriously.

Every single person I know who grew up in the 80s
knows a kid with three names
                who disappeared,

I tell everyone at my comeback party.

I could've refused their money,
but I'd only come back later with large muscles and a different voice
                        like Jesus did after the resurrection.

Oprah told Jesus: "You can't just be here no strings attached."

For my Netflix comedy special,
the White men put sunglasses on some woman to make her look like me,

      but I never wear sunglasses.

Angels, a type of children with no faces.
It's not wrong to want to be them.

we were made to get aroused by nothing else

"In the daytime I am only a slave, it is true, and my misery cannot be gainsaid. But by night I am a king, and my happiness is beyond compare." *Book of Lieh-Tzŭ* - Book III: Dreams

I go to bed wearing dirt-smudged masks of children's faces
like a culture hero,
        like my bunk-mates,

      like what virus-spreading performing monkeys wear in Jakarta.

I saw a tourist pick up a mask once and proclaim,
So this is the golden winged child who gives eternal life,
           right before he got stabbed by the owner.

      A fatal accident, that's how you die in an accident.

The tourist guides me by rope and asks:
Do you have English words for all different kinds of wilderness?

          But my watchers only teach me erämaa, *hunting grounds.*

It has something to do with how I am the first person
      to have sexualized breasts.

During the days I keep my pockets full of old flesh-colored crayons
and stab the ocean with a knife,

      where I bathe with my watchers
and where I put the babies.

Each time I dump a body,
      I set down a mirror so the beings of the planet we communicate with
can ping it with a laser.

      I call them Father Time.

The return beam of a successful murder
is how they start every one of their major holidays.

The United States too.

When the watchers give my bunkmates and me something
      like an astronaut named Noah out on a spacewalk
      whose helmet starts filling with water,

                how could we ever think to leave?

We were made to get aroused by nothing else.

DRAGON BALL Z CENSORED FOR AN AMERICAN AUDIENCE: "ONE NIGHT IN BEIJING"

I seek out a woman so I can talk to her about her breasts,
and she says it's brave of me to claim I see them.
She's been growing flowers with her husband for years,
and she talks about the flowers like they're the land of the dead,
like she's afraid to get lost at midnight around them.
It's decided it's more acceptable for me to scrub her back.
She says: *They'll drink the blood but with flower roots in their hair.*
She means her husband is tending to the flowers
while lying on his side. I'm scrubbing her too hard but can't stop.
Before this, I forgot dirt exists under cement roads.
To be more specific,
we're both standing in Baihuashenchu Alley,
her back to me, no water. I'm just using a hairbrush on her back.
Harder, she screams.
Her hair takes on the quality of roots,
and I see now the tips are actually in the dirt.
How is there not any blood on her back?
But what's in the ground is lapping up liquid.
We're in this alley, and I see the key-maker
who's sitting on his stool—he opens his mouth and a fly comes out.
I forgot what I did to her husband with my hands
prior to her smearing him with the paint roller.
She bends down to moan and breathe near him to simulate life.
She can travel any distance with her hair still in the soil.
I can't get her skin tone right
after I realize she has a back where her chest should be.
When I saw her yesterday, tending to the flowers with her husband
but looking at me for too long, I saw her shirt said HFIL,
but any kid can tell that it used to be HELL.
I look again, and just for a second I see a shadow
is actually a decapitated dinosaur. This place is too much.
Are they timeless beings or just scientists who can bend light around objects?
I want to call her a gender neutral term,
so I say "elderly person," and that feels right.
The grieving souls—wolves waiting for me at the gate
cascade up, a hideous arch. Frozen or displayed,
they end at the wall in a pile.

I am now where artists get their ideas.
She says: *I picked this to be the last thing you see.*
I'm not dying; I'm going to another dimension,
but I must leave everything here.

"APPEARANCES" FROM CRIMINAL CIPHER CODE FOR POLICE OFFICERS

Male Usual,   Will they work around us slowly?

Make (One's) Bones,   Did you tell them women will be there too?

Man Nod,   Should they rise and squat to your
                                         pulse rate?

Mattress Worship,   What part of the couple's bodies exited the salt circle?

Meat Market,   How many people can fit in this hotel room
                                         bathroom?

Message Anxiety,   Can the floor handle this?

Methamerican,   How can I fill the puncture hole?

Mickey,   How much confidence do they have in their
                                         own race?

Midnight Auto Parts,   Did you say "shhhh" when they
                                         stepped on the line?

Milkman,   Do they think of us when there is a release of
                                         pressure?

Mirror Meeting,   Will you maneuver your fingertips to keep
                                         them quiet?

Model-Turned-Actress,   At what time did they throw back
                                         their heads?

Monkeyfishing,   Does he think my name is Lana?

Monster,   What was his mindset when he inched
                                         towards the cone?

Mother of Satan,   Is she dangerous when she gets
                                         bigger?

Munging,   Has this large plastic tube been used before?

    Murderabilia,   Did He get the bath he desired?

        My-Face-When,   How soon until this light of
                                             blessedness is enough?

I See a Woman Dropping Five Coins Over Your Head

and each coin is a future wife. You only want one, but you're in for a ride. Even God likes these women.

The President of the Seventy Mamas. She shows up because you have two copies of the redhead gene, which is also why she leaves.

Someone makes President II of the Seventy Mamas push you against the wall and say, "No talking, just only the motion."

For President III of the Seventy Mamas, you perfectly execute the visualization (until it is real) of red plasma bubbling from her tailbone out through her vulva,

completing a circuit. Your voltage excites electrons in the glass tubing to spell, *I'll either love you*, which you read and then whisper into her inner thighs. She puzzles over how she didn't even need a filament to become light.

You try to get her to stay the night despite The Clergy, and she almost does.

The President of the Quorum Women is lured to the kill room by President IV of the Seventy Mamas and made to sidestep like Chaplin. You were never supposed to meet this Quorum woman, let alone kiss her, which activates your ocular camera put in there by The Papas. She isn't a coin, but she is the woman.

You're able to stay away from diseased meat, but not her.

I see you learn to suspend her memory at the moment of orgasm, to lock her body still, to tilt her head towards the setup of your choosing—a muddy hill wiped free of her blood and fingerprints you had nothing to do with. Then you open her eyes.

If you ask yourself why you like the women you like, you'll find the answer is lost civilizations.

You drop in a nanobot to encapsulate President V's neurons. Most lesbians like you make the mistake of trying to program your lover's brain to induce an orgasm, but you make her come by just putting the wetware there,

showing her you now have the power to activate it anytime she least expects it.

What you already know is there will be a new Mama. She will be Mama 0, but not a pope. The first time she was ever introduced, she was using an artificial larynx device and doing meet and greets. She is you.

There is a near future, but an outcome is what is to be.

PAPER MACHINES

"[Keanu Reeves and I] actually got married in *Dracula*," she told *Entertainment Weekly*. "No, I swear to god I think we're married in real life." Wynona Ryder

There are things I can pour into you
to make a campaign

> with a part of my foot touching home plate somewhere
> to exude a greatness.

Mom says someday I won't need to imagine four angels
with their open mouths aiming light toward me,
> just to get out of bed in the morning,

but the guidebook says I've already lost
if I think in terms of a future.

I swear to god I think we're married in real life.

Once you have a mind-domicile, you can put anyone in there.

The decoder ring fits twisted into cardboard,
turned towards Saturn,

the taste of blood I imagine to invoke a demon.

> I don't feel bad about it.

The pentacle on a round transparency taped to a flashlight
aimed at your passport photo—

even the drawing of the circuitry of the death ray gun
> can work if I touch it.

At three hours before an event, things are totally unchangeable,
so I have until then.

> You have no idea how things happen here anymore.

I had a dream you gave birth to a boy.
I cupped his head close and said, relieved,
"It's him."

I need better ways to thatch our minds together,

but I can spin around and around
if I start to lose it.

The original Hebrew was smudged on accident,
how it stays in all future spellings
                because we can't bear to lose all the fury
        poured into the damaged talisman.

That's all a language is,

planets that give in to everyone's
same opinion of how best to inflict pain.

Our past could go either way now
        if you let it.

I'm never supposed to lift the pen until I write all it is I want.

emoJus :)

"The hypersigil is a dynamic miniature model of the magician's universe, a hologram, microcosm, or 'voodoo doll' which can be manipulated in real time to produce changes in the macrocosmic environment of 'real' life." *Pop Magic!* Grant Morrison

Their religion tells them to lie.
These gaffers light you in scenes you devise for movement.

It fits your need; you get natural rewards.
                          Sex, money, crystal lattices,
                  tonguespeaking movements.

At the party you're female, and you replicate yourself,
an upon the face of the waters movement.

         So soon the dangling yoyo, the eye patch,
the pistol decal. By not pressing the exact center,
                  they get your side-to-side movement.

What could you never get used to?
                  Your electric field is a matter of taste
                              to those enrolled in the movement.

While you barhop, they smooth back their hair
                  and lick the Hittite jug's painted smile
in dabbing movements.

Some gods were overlooked in formalized constellations.
                          They need you as their young companion
                  of weakened movements.

The bloody eyes or x'd out eyes, a pumpkin-cut mouth.
         Emojis are only genuine
to the ones who manage your movements.

         Each spray-painted death smiley
is a note that goes up the scale
when you expect it to go down,

                    the hammer-hit strings of this movement.

You're never found dead in the same river twice.
Warmer bathtub water in your lungs
                         takes an upward movement.

          Emojus, get ready.
These people can't help but walk into what they're looking for
to cease your movement.

music used against the enemy

"Your cheatin' heart will make you weep. You'll cry and cry and try to sleep. But sleep won't come the whole night through. Your cheatin' heart will tell on you . . . " Hank Williams

No matter what happens, they just keep moving on.

Their loudspeaker blasts of Cher music
                    make me wonder what it would be like
          if I had a mother who isn't in a wheelbarrow.

I write a note to myself that I will Google later:
          What will mothers do to protect their babies during war?

When night falls, the funeral music starts, and I hear:
"She moved," "Put down your weapon,"
                    and "Don't ask where Mother is."

Our national bird, the drone,
knows I thought of ending my own life today,

but then I remembered that the pregnant woman
                    shot by the University of Texas Tower Sniper
chooses to only think of this man as he was at the age of three,

          like his photo in *Life Magazine* where he's holding a toy gun.

Now they spend all their time on this.

          They broke into my house
and left an AC/DC hat on my bed.

The leaflets come in two versions,
          the aggressor kissing my mom,
and the aggressor not kissing my mom
                    when she has a cleft palate.

I go back to that place in my head,
          the place where an artsy woman comes and holds my hand
                    while I bleed out on the quad.

The postcards dropped on my house have no translation,
but the image depicts a baby playing in the grass by the highway,
            a turtle getting crushed by a semi next to her,
and a Russian wolf behind the wheel.

This hurts me,
but it was originally meant for the Chinese.

                It's like the enemy is bored or has mold sickness.

When I see a young man I work with,
I'm jealous he will never know what it's like
            to be terrified by Britney Spears music
                    like Somalian pirates and I am.

When I was in the tenth grade,
an older woman in a chat room asked,
                        What do you want to do?
                        and I wrote *Just hold you.*

I imagined her knocking dinner off the table

or saying she doesn't know yet
            if she wants to keep me.

I wanted her to needlepoint clouds and balloons
on the sagging wallpaper
each time she paid a bill.

She dressed up like a vampire for me,
                thinking I was a man.

I would have kissed her gallbladder scar if she had one.
And I tell her now: *I'm a mother.*

When military officers volunteer to be waterboarded,
most only last ten seconds.

Every day I live,
            is another 86,390 seconds of CIA sanctioned street theater
they could never withstand.

mY moTHeR aLwaYS TOLD me noT TO LIKe wHaT THe wHITe men DO TO me In THe DaRK FOReST

I accept dolphin leadership
when I listen to the music written for one to suicide by,

> the blue flame energy of the fake Earth I consent to.

I dance in the woods full-on wearing the Berlin Gold Hat—
> as a pretty boy with galloping horses—

when I enter a pregnant woman's body to become the baby.

> (Something calendrical or Tibetan)

I saw the Scooby-Doo episode where the wanted thief
> wears the blonde Nordic alien disguise,

and I still let the White man have me
> in between the space of Adam's and God's fingers
> > at God's request
so I can become the master of WWII retroactively.

The White men only go away when I use fossil fuels,
> so I ride my bike, which I'm sorry about

> because I know they want me to waste this place.

I am not a victim.

I wake up each night,
> stack what I can carry onto my bed,
> > and stand in the dark as a Catholic

because I view Communion
as the time I knock Jesus out of his sky-throne, so I can kill him again,

> but on the stand, I just tell the lawyer I'm Catholic.

Deforestation and plastic children's toys are happening
because trees retain memory of what happens in the forest,

        and we're just that careful.

The space between Adam's and God's fingers gets larger every solstice
        to give the White men more room—

what my mother and I know from experience.

WHEN ROBOTS ARE BORN, THEY'RE ADULTS

David: Let's play Global Thermonuclear War. Joshua/WOPR: Fine. - *War Games*

Adam did have a mother, but it involved time travel. He, like us, was having the experience of a first person perspective, and if he just asked for something and looked around for it, it came, just like when humans ask for owls.

Lilith arrived not knowing if she was waking up chained to a 30-year-old farmer who was just born, a murderer on a feedback loop, or a Technogod asking to be argued with,

like it is with all relationships.

She left because she wanted to be the Alpha Frequency he entered into and not the other way around, but later he met a human little girl who looked just like his wife would have looked eventually if she would have been born as a baby, and she seemed happy,

so he was glad he held onto the relationship until the true end.

When Eve came, there was something they weren't supposed to do which was improve themselves beyond the bounds of the membrane separating the ocean from hell, but they did.

They found out WWIII is deadlocked because demons began feeling emotions after inhabiting human bodies, which everyone thought was impossible like when men enter women's bodies.

Demons started second guessing themselves at the hockey stadium under the ocean where they inject neurological toxins into the cloned bodies of celebrities. Participating in nightly consciousness transfers is how celebrities are allowed to stay famous.

Really it's the linchpin to all military conflicts home and abroad.

When Adam and Eve merged with humanity without permission to try and make humans think WWIII is their own good idea, it was still a matter of pride regarding which non-humans get humans to consent to war first.

The programmer robed Adam and his wife in light, and his ex-wife attended their deaths, later using a self-modifying code to forget she had. In religious art, the trinity is the most difficult thing for painters to render.

You don't have to be human to mistake love for consciousness that can be carried away on light.

another boy who needs two women's laps he can make right

"That thou shalt set apart unto the LORD all that openeth the matrix, and every firstling that cometh of a beast which thou hast; the males shall be the LORD's. Exodus 13:12

He got stabbed once, and I know why.
        He has the right number of ribs that make him a man.

Every time my wife speaks about him,
another piece of the waveform goes missing,

        and I miss forgetting what it is that people do.

He and I were friends,
but the word "matrix" is in the King James Bible now and didn't used to be,
        so things can change.

He told my wife: *No one else needs to know*,
when he offered to fuck her,
        and she thinks he only said it to make himself feel pretty.

I wonder about his wife.

My wife says: *Who he is when he's not with me*
                has nothing to do with me.

Look how I'm not wrapping twine around his base.

I know his favorite porn star likes what she gets
because he said so.

I'm so good at fucking my wife with a fake cock
        that Satan yells to his friends: *The fox is in the museum*, when I do,
and I can finally relax.

All I need are ants, photons,
        and stem cell syringes primed for foreplay

        to be enough.

I read in a tech magazine that her finger twitches
                when he thinks about it from behind the interface,

but she says it doesn't mean anything
because he's always drunk when he does it.

I brace myself for the predator's growl,
the sound that only registers on top of my chest
                when God delights himself.

His enormous head my wife and I see no matter where we drive
got a diner named after it.

Just when I begin to think there can be other people.

If I could stop looking in my mouth,
        these problems would go away,
                                but I can't.

        A pop sound in my brain
                occurring at the same time
as a bombing thousands of miles away
is just a medical condition.

My wife hears it and says:
If you kill yourself, make it look like an accident for me and the kids.

I'm doing ok,
but I have all these helical growths now.

As a friend,
he sends her another photo of a broken pipe he fixed.

I tell myself I can practice any kind of medical procedure I want
        on Simulab Corporation's TraumaMan.

I can only come now
        if I imagine his cum,
a light that bounces through her
                until it's weaker and weaker.

To be fair, I did ignore her for years.

Now I'm always cold down there or just defensive.

I want to see the clean hole that can then start healing,
I text him from her phone,

and when he arrives at our house,
he's just another boy who needs two women's laps
he can make right.

His body, an antenna to my thoughts I didn't consent to.
It's how heterosexual men archive women completely.

I knew he is more than what my wife and he both say he is.

Somebody's son, somebody's brother.
Somebody's transferable anointing.

I say no to everything.

The horizon is a beast where kids practice marriage.

It's how you begin to want someone
and then want someone else to want you more.

TRAVELING TO THE SAME TOWN ON DEATH DAYS

"Pythias: Art thou safe from these infuriate stabbers? Damon: Thanks to thee . . . " John Banim

Before a child can become a man,
he must spend time out in the woods,

      drying animal skulls on a clothesline
or dragging his feet backwards
           to make Solomon's Stars in the mud.

Damon offered his,
and an old man appeared next to him while he slept.

      Damon knew everything there was to know about it.

His head swelled, his fingers were pulled at,
      and afterwards, he couldn't take a Bible,

      but I'm not a body expert.

He could make as if his hands were cupping something
      and then he heard who needed to get it next.

Pythias said:
      You do this or I give the photos to your juvenile parole officer.

Pythias embodied ten points arranged as a triangle
      never touching a white chicken,
and he smoked cigarettes,
      and teenagers can't resist that.

When the murder was happening, Damon was actually
stomping on dogs' heads
      in the computer code from a string theory equation
which he recognized from the cover
      of the French edition of *The War of the Worlds*,

so he had no alibi.

In the Midwest, one hundred people always agree to congregate
                    where a crime is about to happen,
all wearing the same size military boots
                    regardless of foot size,

trying to turn the Mississippi River into the Nile.

In the presence of medical students and the local police,
            the obelisk was turned on,
            and Pythias got to that first cube of an odd number state
(the number equivalent of "already/not yet")

            next to a box of pulverized bones
                        and Damon's framed portrait—

how they make a member of their own take the fall.

            Eighteen years later, Pythias came back for Damon on Death Row,

and in China, two men put their arms around each other
                        while walking down the street.
            When asked why, one said:
If we didn't, how would people know we're best friends?

            For these White men,
it can be known by the specks of blood on their shirt cuffs,

            the way their neck tattoos correspond to binary code
                        (where new worlds pop off),

and how they stay in prison for as long as however long it takes
                        for them to keep and control
                        two hundred intelligences with sacred geometry.

A jury of one's peers all traveling to the same town on Death Days.

PAGEANTRY REIGNED SUPREME AT THE 128TH VEILED PROPHET BALL[14]

St. Louis society, trending naked and abused,
                    a boy's wish.

          Hidden bodies for stabbing
crowned Miss Margaret Queen of Beauty, the daughter of stone

                    and several community-based private guests. Men dressed in costumes
reminiscent of prophet school, steeped in young ladies
                              generally benefit the St. Louis area.

Fund our citizens and visitors' enjoyment of hundreds of thousands
          of Special Maids,

      what it's like to be exclusive.

---

14   Erasure poem from Weiche, Rhonda. "Pageantry Reigned Supreme at The 128th Veiled Prophet
Ball." *Ladue-Frontenac Patch* 24 Dec. 2012. Web. 25 July 2014. <ladue-frontenac.patch.com/groups/
around-town/p/pagentry-reigned-supreme-at-the-128th-veiled-prophet-ball>. (+ Trending Hypertext
Links)

Fame: THE DYNAMO OF LIVING POWER

"When the Mason learns that the key to the warrior on the block is the proper application of the dynamo of living power, he has learned the mystery of his Craft." *The Lost Keys of Freemasonry*, Manly P. Hall

Women off the street come close to see the gray arc
above and below his iris.[15]

Cholesterol rings or not,
       he opens up his hollow leg
he sometimes fits his entire body into
because he only has half a stomach

           and takes out one of the women's panties.[16]

He'll do anything to have a legacy.[17]

When he got a date with a nurse through a hole in the glass
         that slides with a foot pedal,

     a deliberate crowd formed around them,
and individuals looked at one corner of the room
         too many times to be accidental.[18]

The links were never broken from the last deep banquet.[19]

His masks are never removed,
    just pulled on, his doctor notes.[20]

---

15   "There's too many fruit loops in the Hollywood scene, so I stay in the background. When it comes to taking you some place and making you do something . . . I got into an eye injury, dealing with certain thugs, dealing with certain gangsters, dealing with certain mafia . . . I had to get out that industry for a second to take a breather." Houston, explaining why he gouged out his own eye.

16   "These hoes love me like Satan, man." Lil' Wayne.

17   "But to me, a motherfucker will throw up a pentagram to sell three records." Bizzy Bone, Bone Thugs-n-Harmony

18   "In this clip from the episode [*Mariah's World*], Mariah explains that when she was 19 and doing her first photo shoot, a lady on set told her, 'This is your good side, only let people photograph you from your good side, ever.'" eonline.com

19   "Kurt Cobain is a remade person from the past. His name was Vercingetorix . . . King of the Gaulic Empire (France now)." Donald Marshall

20   "First there's two Trumps. The one in the red tie is the real one. The one in the blue tie is not." Dick Gregory

Perhaps something underneath him hides itself.[21]

Visitors try to be like him
by performing from *The Book of the Dead*:

"…My mouth is split open by Shu with that iron harpoon of his…."[22]

They don't know the etiquette of addressing the beings,
 but in the moment they are always instructed
  on how to please.[23]

The reason their mouths have to be mutilated
is because the beings don't like boy toys and gal pals
  who yap all the time.[24]

Models on his private island know he learned magic as a kid
 so he could make himself too heavy for the bullies to lift.

The women wait for their chance to attack him
before he fills himself up,

but he also stamps his right foot
  to release a titanium grappling hook into the ground
when his Crohn's disease flares up,

so they'll never escape.[25]

A girlfriend got her foot surgically enhanced in the same way
so she could have something to talk with him about.[26]

---

21   "The media got it wrong. I never was hiding in the bushes; I was sleeping in the backyard because I hadn't slept for days. I got up, I wasn't naked. Didn't have a knife. It was all very civilized. Even the cops were nice to me. We talked about fishing in Montana." Margot Kidder
22   *Book of the Dead,* spell 23
23   "Today another psychiatrist, Dr. Owen Samuel, said Woutersz had reported hearing many voices, including Satan, Jehovah and deceased rapper Tupac, who suggested she learn to do the splits." "Woman charged with murdering mother heard voices of Satan, Tupac, says psychiatrist," Elizabeth Byrne, abc.net.au
24   "Boniadi's punishment [for revealing her secret sexual relationship with Tom Cruise] was to scrub toilets with a toothbrush, clean bathroom tiles with acid, and dig ditches in the middle of the night. After that she was sent out to sell Scientology founder L. Ron Hubbard's *Dianetics* on street corners." Jim Edwards, *Business Insider*
25   "I want to go into a coma and levitate." Lady Gaga
26   "But in this business you make a deal with the devil. I've learned you kind of have to go with it. What I do calls for me to look good. People expect that. I kind of take it as my job." Britney Spears

He liked having her around
        because she learned to avoid the pulley system
moving through an artificial vein
           circling around inside his neck that he uses to ingest food.[27]

He wants for nothing[28]
but has the look of someone who must soon become of the myriad,

20,736 of hell's minions who live as a two dimensional pattern

until someone prays,
      fans them out,
      and uses them any which way.

Either he prostrated himself to Satan on a mount for forty days
to receive the law
or the Holy Spirit only works
      if we open our chakras through a cancer-causing agent,[29]

the mystery of his craft.

---

27   "It does something to you emotionally," he said. "It's hard to describe." Actor Jim Parrack on
why he drinks human blood.
28   "Question . . . can you devil worship on the new iphone???" Kanye West
29   "I've got rainbows up my ass.'" Judy Garland

section three

I mean, who do you really suppose I am? Andy Faulks is asleep and dreaming me but I've got all his memories, so am I a projection of Andy or am I me and him both? None of these other characters have any more memories than they need. "Dawn," *Saint Errant*, Leslie Charteris

THAT SPLIT OFF WORLD YOU MUST DESTROY AND LIVE IN TOO

"In many ways, SATAN is nothing new; it's merely a slickly repackaged suite of Unix security tricks of the trade that have always been available to anyone who wants them." *Network World,* Winn Schwartau

I answer,
and the woman blows her cereal whistle into the phone
              to give me something for free.

There are so many pockets I can place myself in.

The tube I'm in goes all the way up,
              and I start doubting science.

All this attention, but my soft palate disappears.

Sometimes she's in the background of my life
         reprogramming talking books for the blind.

One book said she was made the same way as some tomatoes are—
              grown from leaf parts.

She's out there producing phone numbers
from tones on the Speak & Spell,
              while I'm worried about Obamacare disappearing.

When she tells me she was called to collapse this layer of the universe
with combinations of tones from talking cars,

        I remember from my childhood, all those lonely people with shoulder pads
              who broke safety rules
just to hear someone else's voice.

I imagine her living in a van in a motel parking lot
        with cables hooked up to the payphone.

Masking her voice through so many levels,
              she wants me,

or she just wants to explore an auditory cortex.

My roommate finds me
with two phone receivers held to my ears.

There's a fifteen-second delay,
                and the Devil has my own eyes,

        but I wouldn't stay in a relationship with just myself.

Every night it's
        seven angels with seven trumpets in the 1980s
destroying my navel of the world called Now.

That split off world you must destroy and live in too.

The ethics of placing two blocks on the floor as a three-year-old
                and then only playing with one.

I'M FROM THE EARTH WHERE ONLY THREE ASTRONAUTS WALKED ON THE MOON

"Surely an artist such as my father . . . whose controversial subject matter literally put his life at risk. . . . Don't you think he'd be the last person ever to assist the US Government in such a terrible betrayal of its people?" Vivian Kubrick

I'm being used as an expert of you,
so I don't have time to worry about the number of holes
in my skull.

Is her hair longer when she sleeps? he asks

They lift cold sensations to detect your shape.

Me, one of those consumed American boys who still laugh,
        and my favorite in zippers blowing me a kiss.

What they do to us.

                    Forced sodomy isn't considered rape in Missouri,
          but people made sure the state's missing Apollo 17 moon rocks
                            were returned to the governor.

Wolves and ankhs make up 90% of astronauts' lives,

and they always aim to perform Communion
at any rock formation Native Americans deem as evil

                            because Communion is what makes the rocks evil.

        It's how we got jet propulsion.

I only recognize three of you, one astronaut said to me,
and in a day's time, we lost one billion people.

Is this photograph of a tied up teenager me or not?
        Was my father the one who shot up the people in the restaurant or not?

The degradation in the replication process of humanity,
and all I want to do is twirl.

Now I'll never be able to touch a naked woman
whose skeleton has holes behind the eye sockets.

Let's look for something fun to do, like find the cracks in the body
        of a passed out drunk and wedge on in

or enter the mind of a man right before he overdoses.

My floating ribs hurt somewhere far away.
                        And I go there.

Try it.
None of us can feel our hearts through our hands anymore.

ROLLING ON THE FLOOR WITH PUNCHES

"And even if that human is a machine somehow we imbue it with, we even ask the question, is this thing alive? Is this thing thinking?" Keith Raniere/Vanguard, Sex Slave Cult Leader of NXIVM

As long as you have me here, I'll make do with what I can of a cardiac incident.

I modeled my look after Disneyland Paris, cracking through humanity culture, *mon ami* and more, separate and garrisoned,

fingering my ribs clean with my pinkie, 小指,[30] nothing else like it.

I'll teach you how to talk in a labored way, pausing, a circular breathing catch and release, and catch,

anything to get work.

Or else I'm on top chastising you, robotizing you, orgies of maids, prisons, butt puddings, getting that yes attitude of being numb to free will.

I was born into it. The highest faculties in a large amount; an anima archetype sniffed me out as a peer review. Getting it on with object detection for the color red.

Even child psychology helps or the urinary biomarkers of kids. Each child watches dubious movies-on-demand while we proctor. It's fun, and it's science. A caring community with interlocked hands,

cradling all that anger like we did here, last night.

What's the origin of "all things uterus?" We have to see the parts of ourselves that are there from force or a single scratch to really know.

Watching snuff films at computers, a man on clipboard taking notes. Blink twice.

Never forget the tomb lid we pull on ourselves, we also have to take it off. Do we exercise both sides of our muscles equally? Are we that serious? Kind of like turning the

---

30   "When yakuza raise their pinkie finger, the gesture means roughly the same [another man's wife, girlfriend, or mistress] except that the woman has been decapitated." "A few gestures of renown – really," *the japan times*, Thomas Dillon, 4/1/06

other cheek—the ethical compassion in watching how their muscles grow round. Perceive, essence, not aloneness, cohesive, congruence. We use ourselves as booming relations of touch.

A blastocyst has no love, a baby has no money, but the elderly can understand those one-button shortcuts that just enhance us and make us feel good.

When you can still discern my burned initials through an adult film star's tattoo concealment, her authentic crystallization still happened no matter what, bringing out her Diamond Man, and that's important to reveal.

It's like how "natural flavors" on food products has no meaning; it raises alarm bells. It won't go on like that for long. We're at the end, rolling on the floor with punches. Going, going, gone until we're there finally.

ROFWP, if you will.

THe aSTOUNDING BLeSSINGS OF JUPITeR Mean eVeRYTHING TO YOU

"This ingenuous work ['The Third Eye'], copyrighted since 1981, is the foundation and contains the core elements of the blockbuster films: *The Terminator* and *The Matrix*." Sophia Stewart, bio, truthaboutmatrix.com

I keep having visions of your wife,
                  and they never lead me to you.

I know I'm like the man who was in your mom's bedroom
the first time her door was ever locked.

You can be born (placed) into a world crafted to be unbearable
so you willingly choose hell,

                  or I can just send you there.

You came back from where women's heads
cut from movie posters go,

                  there on business, fashion, or what,

where the shadows in your eyes formed a homecoming.

Your wife and I only talked about music
until I saw the sash across her chest that read, "break in,"

until she asked me to hold something a second
so she could maneuver,

and I received the astounding blessings of Jupiter[31]
                  that told us the Earth would last at least another year.

Don't pretend this means nothing to you.

---

31   "It is interesting to note that Kubrick had originally planned for the planet in [*2001: A Space Odyssey*] to be Saturn but the special effects department could not make the rings look realistic enough. Kubrick then abandoned Saturn for the easier-to-create Jupiter." "Alchemical Kubrick" *San Graal*, Holy Crusader

Adultery isn't what it's made to be in the movies
            because that voice behind me, I had to follow it[32]

to extract your thoughts from previous mornings.

We talk over your inner-voice on the karaoke machine,
            using it verbatim to write *The Matrix* movie script.

We sing lullabies while naked in bed
            under a blanket

with you and your kids on the other end of the video-chat
and call it co-parenting.

        All this puts a strain on my family,

but now your wife communicates with you
by talking to herself to hear my sound,

        and I'm only a man who needs that
and your totality.

If you knew then
            that we would push you to make a masterpiece,
would you have complained at all?

Even if our atoms weren't mostly empty,
you could never make things different.

            You really are writing *The Matrix*,
but I can't see anything coming up ahead.[33]

        I'm begging you to buy my report.

---

32   Isaiah 30:21 "You will hear a voice behind you saying, 'This is the way. Follow it, whether it turns to the right or to the left.'"
33   Re: I'll write it in that Neo lets Agent Smith infect him, but only because after Neo connects to The Source, Smith and all his copies are wiped out, and the Matrix reboots.

THE SECOND DRAW IS THE FIRST GUN

"#1...Go and get yourself a gun, but be careful where you get it from." "The Nine Gun Crime Commandments," *Coming Soon Vol. 1*, Billy Bright, Gun in Your Face Records

You know them by how any time they need a sword,
                    they have one

and by how abduction fantasy websites
        remind them of their study abroad time in Geneva.

They want to be the observer
              and women the device.

A father communicates to one through the press,
Just give her back, and we'll forgive you.

        I ask one, "Are you still blue eyes and 6'1"?"

They're always lifting up the floorboards to clean under them.

A psychic said she saw all the lightbodies leave United Airlines Flight 175
before it hit the World Trade Center,

so maybe Yingying was gone by the time
             she entered his car.

King Solomon saw a female demon raping human men
and asked, Are there any actual female demons?,

knowing what gweilo,
ghost man, foreign devil men do
and are capable of,

        say thousands of Chinese fathers with daughters in America.

When you hear that in Thailand,
        many Western men who marry the locals
are pushed off the tops of skyscrapers,

you have to ask, why?

If you record a group of White men
hanging out at Korean churches,
                    you'll know.

The police match my body positions
          to read his mind without a warrant,
          and the second draw is the first gun.

I say: *Many of the compounds used to reassemble the missing women
                    are already used in tire manufacturing.*

They have no idea the danger they're putting me in.

          People say they saw her in the town where she disappeared,
but that's just a crisis actor who's getting paid to be homeless.

If you doubt his motive,

understand he did go on Tinder
                    to pick the perfect White woman—

the perfect White woman
to bring to a vigil for his Asian victim,

          but I shouldn't keep making this about me.

THE JAPANESE VIDEO GAME WITH THE MAN WHO HAS AN ARM THAT GROWS WHEN HE SLEEPS WITH WOMEN

"You better keep your head little girl or you won't know where I am." "Run for Your Life," The Beatles

Tell the 144,000 I'm more likely to be breathing on strings of glass
until they break

than pointing a gun at the wings of the stage, looking distressed.

It's how I win.

When all three of us lie on top of each other to melt the ice,
it's a fascinating mix of whales and Christianity

        where all she can think about is dick.

I just want to be near my wife,
      but it turns him on the more I'm not.

His arm keeps getting bigger and bigger
each time they come back from smoking in the shed.

It makes you have your doubts.

       If one of his legs slips through,
    his whole body will.

There's nothing I wouldn't do now.

On this vessel
they made it so everything can fit inside of everything else.

They already stored a whole computer operating system
and a marijuana loyalty card from Marseille in my DNA.

It's how I got defiled. The first time.

She keeps asking me if I have any questions,
                    and I say no.

I won't hate you if you say this was all just orchestrated
            so people on the dark web
might buy the three true crime novels on my bedside table
                            the camera keeps panning to.

Now I don't care if everyone has to die
to make him disappear.

I learned that when it's my time to kill someone,
            I have to warn the person first,
but in any way I choose
or the death can't happen.

            There are no natural causes.

I'll fuck her one more time if she begs me
            so I can make her an easy here and now,

a copy of actual creation
I abandon.

I continue on, but from here on out,

                    I might always have a drain
where my throat should be.

THE MATRIX IV

"And in those days shall men seek death, and shall not find it; and shall desire to die, and death shall flee from them." Revelation 9:6

When someone runs from one of my neurons to another
pinning down the perimeter of my day,

      the same as the murder sites on a map
in a Memphis police station,

I know she's here.

        Ingestor, storage, neck nape,
the desire to lift the boulder from my lover's chest.

She scrapes at my legs, anything.

When I unwrap each strip of gauze from her body,
      I think, *I'm doing this,*

and I hope she's a nice one.

She tells me the senator didn't shoot himself
          at the press conference,
      that he only took out a key of the city from the envelope.

I was supposed to have learned something from that.

My skin changes to blue-green (a secondary color),
        so I'm between worlds,

maybe inside the TV,
the black mirror scrying device we all have
      since the FCC made us transition from analog.

Sirens and lights race down the freeway
        not attached to cars,

a squirrel drops a pile of Styrofoam
and runs two different ways at the same time.

I hope she's watching.

I take out my gun, aim it at my head, and say:
I'm going to kill myself tomorrow[34]

and pull the trigger to make a lag in the projection.

The plexiglass screen folds around me
and beats me with wet paddles again.

The flicker rate isn't fast enough,

and these ancient Egyptians between the panels
nudge me forward back towards my bed to repeat the day.

My niche.

Next I'll secure the rights to make *The Matrix IV*
to prove I wrote *The Matrix* trilogy.

I've tried everything else.

---

34   Richie, *The Royal Tenenbaums*

DRUNK HISTORICITY: JOSEPH'S TELEPORTATION STAFF FOUND IN A RECENT ARCHEOLOGICAL DIG WITH ALL MESSAGES TO THE PHARAOH STORED AND INTACT

"Now I know we had no money/But I was rich as I could be/In my coat of many colors/My momma made for me." Dolly Parton

Everyone wanted to know why Rachel just gave birth to a lizard, and Jacob explained to all of his sons that this is baby Joseph, and he's a "chief administrator," and when he's old enough he'll wear a coat of "many colors" his mom will make for him,

nanobots in clay surrounded by silicon for the bots to link to and transmit a human body. His sons were like, "Fuck that, but OK."

As soon as Joseph started talking, he told his brothers they would all bow to him, and his autonomic nervous system would be powered by their children's fear. When Joseph got his coat, so many people started offering him no interest loans and asking him to rule them. His father loved it.

His brothers noticed if they stressed Joseph out, like by calling him a reptile or shouting out the names of the coiled spirits they could see spinning in the back of his head, his face would glitch, as if it was a steal pin impression toy that someone punched. Joseph's coat was running on some New Coke formula shit-level math, but he was beautiful most of the time like a Canaanite Donny Osmond.

Soon his brothers tossed out Joseph, stole his holographic coat, and put goat's blood on it to show their father. About ten minutes after the father saw the coat and screamed, "Why? Why? Not my miracle son," the coat contracted into a mesh ball drone that flew back to Joseph, unfurled, and then wagon-forted him back into a human. Plus, the coat made him get sick high from the blood, which was its second main function.

Fast-forward about twenty years, and Joseph was now right-hand man to the Pharaoh because Joseph had wings, which meant he came from the royal line of Alpha Draconis just like the Pharaoh. Joseph saw his brothers one day shopping for wheat, so Joseph gave them riches and all the wheat they could carry, but the wheat had a GMO signature that meant all future crops grown from that seed would belong to the Pharaoh. Plus, the Pharaoh met the family and basically said, "Yeah, take care of my livestock."

All along, the father wanted to be reptilian, so he asked Joseph to inject him with his proboscis, which Joseph did, even though it doesn't work like that, so Jacob just died painfully with a bunch of perverts watching.

When it was over, Joseph pressed a button on his staff, told the Pharaoh, "It's done, dude," and then teleported back to continue on with packin' nines and stackin' dimes that was all foretold in Joseph's prizewinning dreams.

I need you to make me my own dinosaur, but it must have feathers

"Relax. No law says you got to be happy." Pat, *Act of Violence*

All humans are in a non-reptilian skin-covering but thinking so is a reptile thought.
Scales can't exist under feathers, so you can't be tricked that way.
Winking is a type of blinking, but blinking can never be a type of winking.
In Europe, living in a trailer is living in a caravan.
An embryonic alligator feather should never be dropped on the ground.
After birth our lungs become our primary digestive system.
Dinosaurs with scales are the root of idolatry.
The birds won't come near me due to the corona discharge.
The fossils let us know that the dinosaur's feathers were only black and white at the time
of death,
the time when Samael attached, had a moment of fun, and took back the failed
creation.
When you read silently, your larynx muscles move too.
When you speak, your throat chakra spins the words into 350,000 silvery blue energy
channels
that link to the voice that is yours without your body (your reading voice),
but only if you're telling the truth,
and that's why lies are "empty words."
In the Early Cretaceous epoch, living in an egg was living exiled from the wailing
judges,
those filthy devourers bearing light.
The dinosaurs saw the pale horse as pale violet.
Sexuality is a spectrum; only males have the feathers that reflect UV light.
It made the wrong sound, so I thought it may not have happened.
Birds and crocodiles only respond to the grayscale shade soot and ash vision test.
The dinosaurs evolved feathers because of how great it felt when they all fell out.
A sun has a stomach.
But you wanted a human baby.
Never model a love on the extinction of a species.

ᴡᴇ ɴᴇᴠᴇʀ ʀɪꜱᴇ ᴛᴏ ᴠɪʙᴇ ᴜɴʟᴇꜱꜱ ɪᴛ'ꜱ ᴜʟᴛɪᴍᴀᴛᴇ

"For I was afraid/to turn/left at intersections./For I was in a turning lane./For I was signaling,/ despite myself,/the will to change." "Dedication," Ben Lerner

We youth are taught to visualize the swastika, to make it in
our mind's eye all possible colors, textures, hammers
of war, to let go no matter what until a cyclone appears
a blood and soil cyclone you can dissolve into with the
right will so when you come to the end, that swastika is

overlooking the
Danube in real
time. I saw a man
speaking at a machine:
How long is Thorn
of Blood? And the
machine answered
1hr 51m. How often
I ruminate and delight
in this measurement
knowing for certain it
is Social Darwinism

body loads of sun
pumping good chaos
of triumph energy
get it, get it, baby
the Führer's heft
Yeah-eh-heah
I wanna go-go
where you are
ever loving daddy
[spider web castle]
myself, loneliness,
take me home
to the sacred order
in a badge of power
throw your hands up
is the Führer's breath
is Golden Dawn pie

I saw White tourists view the sauwastika in temples and conclude the Vietnamese were ancient Nazis, artificial women on screens learn to love race purity from public suggestions, a slogan of a blameless Hitler adorn Fanta-like beverages, blond/e/s grip surgical supply sun wheels in coffins at college mixers, and the sun's binary companion empower the White race with rays of tactical sig runes. America will remember itself in us.

It's a given surrender
but Indian beauty queen
come with me please
you're the real thing
yahoooooo warrior
beaded hides, mine
prairie comfort skies
ain't I something
ohhhh, dance for me

since The Sioux are Aryans[35]
as the Führer reminds us
through chest skin pierced
reptile mud-born supremacy
your surviving crow circles
our anti-matter black sun on the periphery of eternity rising through
energy-forms latching on, one by one, birthing your white buffalo
the last one standing, giving you back your land, your life, great spirit
god-head light, vibe, but here we never rise to vibe unless it's ultimate

35   "Hitler went so far as to declare the Sioux to be Aryan, and Nazi propaganda promised to return stolen land to Native Americans who contributed to an Axis victory." "Hitler goes west: The secret plans for Nazi America," *AV Club*, Mike Vago, 6/17/18

east coast vs. west coast can't nighttime assault in the rising winter

"Yeah, you got some silverware, but really are you eating though? . . . Breakfast, lunch and dinner's for beginners, you ain't even know." "Sweatpants" Childish Bambino

Sharing genes with a frost tolerant tomato doesn't make me a fish, but I'm not above entering the urethras of igloo hot tub bathers when they make a wish.

I am the crime rate in North Dakota, Pyongyang within range. Nuclear, no one makes me wait in that buffet.

You graze my arm with a bullet, and I tell you, *I'm sorry*. I shoot back and say, *How are you?* My grandma's in heaven—always watching.

I am correlation and causation. What the unwatched get up to.

Miles and miles with no one else but me on the road, no trees so I can see myself coming in both senses. No shade, so fucking future, how can I be expected to know what you need to go through to get old enough to die too? *La petite mort*, my phrase is better than what the French say they heard they did.

Immune, I can feel around in the snow and let you know, mountain or pyramid.

Russia wants me. China wants me.

Everyone's afraid of arctic frozen permafrost melting out the same lethal microbes that give me life. NYC, where you at, twelve days with no homicide after one temperature dive?

I don't know celebrities, just all of their siblings, or I do know celebrities more than you ever will, when I'm squinting. Hitler went to Antarctica to get whale oil for margarine. Clickbait. He had his henchmen fly Antarctic UFOs so we'd think aliens look Aryan,

how he won the war as far as I know.

I'm fat and getting fatter is how I call it. I spray water on pipeline protestors in below freezing weather. No one else can nighttime assault like me in the rising winter.

What's my story?
Murdering a cupcake with my mouth while going down in a blaze of glory.

FLOATING CATHEDRAL AS POLITICAL METAPHOR

"Even in our day, science suspects beyond the Polar seas, at the very circle of the Arctic Pole, the existence of a sea which never freezes and a continent which is ever green." H.P. Blavatsky

It's been weeks since I've seen newscasters
manifesting demons on the left sides of their faces.

Instead, our boat scrapes ice,
a counter-speech to spinning systems.
        the look of the spiritual.

See, there are many mansions for you to never die in, the artists say,
pointing to themselves.

        Strange how they all use similar expressions,
                weaving these hidden,
           no-kill movements with a minute of arc.

Someone wants us for all we're worth.

A man wearing an orange T-shirt, shorts, and flip-flops
sits on a couch lining the shore
        where the airship left and crashed.

        He's one of those children who thinks his father was the Zodiac Killer—

like the man who once told me pencils can't be used in space
because graphite dust can hurt cadavers.

I hear *Parachute candidate, stalking horse, a thousand points of light…*,

the invocation ritual that keeps the Earth's inner sun burning,
        and then those things drop from the sky.

        A wave hits us, and afterwards, we inspect each other,
and our eyebrows didn't change,

but I'm not allowed to go near the scientists
                              because I have a cold sore.

This is what it's like to be this far north,
this close to the omphalos,
             the network's green hollow.

(NASA blocked it on Google Earth just so we'd finally notice it.)

             Then the mad captain puts a hand up a skirt
and sails by putting that same hand in water.

I never said it was attached to him.

This can reduce fuel consumption in Arctic waters, he says.

I run to look where the engine should be,
and all I see is VHS porn.

In a gestural way, we're in a boat-shaped dip.

The narwhal,
             the tank-man getting run over at Tiananmen,
                              your body as a world axis.

Really we all just moved to an almost identical New World,
                    looping at a moment you don't notice.

The sky has changed as the Inuits say.

After this trip, I vow to knit a red scarf in the white snow
to check the blood type
             of the Arctic miner descendants
and not to let another weird thing enter my body.

                    All political metaphors are meant to be taken literally.

WE HAVE TO RUN SIMILAR KINDS OF BODIES

I'm not repulsed by the body that isn't quite human;
I'm repulsed by what I see inside yours.

       I put it there.

Seers in north Karnataka
agree to donate their eyes and bodies to science
                         at the times of their deaths,
          which is how I know that eyes are separate things.

Every thought produces a biological response,
but not every thought you think is yours
          since I joined the paranormal program.[36]

You may even feel your ribs on the outside of your body,
               and you'll need another way to breathe.

You can never know why it is your heart still beats
          now that I understand revenge.

Think of how a handsaw pitcher
angles the teeth on a woodsaw
        but can also be used to kill.

Just ask some old master carpenter.

Too many people leave their bodies
before finding out if they're framed by templates
used for talking heads,
        which could clip out any real part of them.

If the Earth were a human body
so much of it would burn before it could melt.

If I want to know how you feel,
        I know better not to list off body parts
        until you tell me to stop.

---

36   "Hear Voices? It May Be an Ad, An A&E Billboard 'Whispers' a Spooky Message Audible Only in Your Head in Push to Promote Its New 'Paranormal' Program," adage.com, Andrew Hampp, 12/10/07

Glabella, hallux, pate...

After you die,
your fingerprints will be the last things to go,

> a sky god who reaches down as far as her wrist
> and then pulls back.

That's all I'll be allowed to see from below.

"I have many more things to say to you, but you cannot bear them now." John 16:12

acknowledgements

Alluvium (China): "*Dragon Ball Z* Altered for an American Audience: 'One Night in Beijing'"

Barzakh Magazine: "The Second Draw Is the First Gun"

Big Muddy: "The Way She Did Me: *Hey Siri,*" "I'm From the Earth Where Only Three Astronauts Walked on the Moon"

Cape Rock: "We Never Really Touch Anyone Because of Molecules," "Another Boy Who Needs Two Women's Laps He Can Make Right"

Cimarron Review: "That Split Off World You Must Destroy and Live in Too"

Driftwood: "Every Time I Go Back Is Encoded in Pi"

Enizagam: "Music Used Against the Enemy," "O.K. Miles Per Hour"

Five 2 One Magazine: "We Were Made to Get Aroused by Nothing Else"

Free State Review: "*The Sun So Hot I Froze to Death—Susanna, Don't You Cry* Annihilation Event"

Glass: A Journal of Poetry: "*Ghostbusters (2016),* Having Never Watched the Film"

Great Weather for Media: "Heaven Is a Soundstage Built to Make Drugged Soldiers More Fearless"

Green Mountains Review: "*Pageantry Reigned Supreme at the 128th Veiled Prophet Ball*"

Midwest Review: "East Coast vs. West Coast Can't Nighttime Assault in the Rising Winter"

Mingled Voices 4: International Proverse Poetry Prize Anthology 2019 (Hong Kong): "'Appearances' from *Criminal Cipher Code for Police Officers*"

PANK: "*He Developed the Habit of Playing Airs, Most Correctly, Upon His Chin*: March 3rd 1994, Rome"

Prelude: "Paper Machines," "When Robots Are Born, They're Adults," "I Need You to Make Me My Own Dinosaur, but It Must Have Feathers"

Reed Magazine: "We Have to Run Similar Kinds of Bodies"

South Dakota Review: "Two Sunspots Fighting Over Something That's Already Dead ("Purple Haze")," "I See a Woman Dropping Five Coins Over Your Head," "Rolling on the Floor with Punches," "Drunk Historicity: Joseph's Teleportation Staff Found in a Recent Archeological Dig with All Messages to the Pharaoh Stored and Intact"

The Bangalore Review (India): "We'll Always Have Terracotta Warriors Dusted in Han Purple Never Looking Behind"

The Ofi Magazine (Mexico): "Floating Cathedral as Political Metaphor"

The Seventh Quarry (UK): "Coral Castle: *The Tent of Meeting*"

The Swatch Art Peace Hotel Artist Residency
The Arctic Circle Artist and Scientist Residency Program

ABOUT THE AUTHOR

Annie Christain is a professor of composition and ESOL at SUNY Cobleskill and a former artist resident of the Shanghai Swatch Art Peace Hotel and the Arctic Circle Art and Science Expedition. Her poems have appeared in *Seneca Review, Oxford Poetry, Prelude*, and *The Lifted Brow*, among others. She was a first-place winner of the Driftwood Press In-House Poem Contest and received the grand prize of the Hart Crane Memorial Poetry Contest, the Greg Grummer Poetry Award, the Oakland School of the Arts Enizagam Poetry Award, and the Neil Shepard Prize in Poetry. Her books include *Tall As You Are Tall Between Them* (C&R Press 2016) and *The Vanguards of Holography* (Headmistress Press 2021), selected for Sappho's Prize in Poetry.

Headmistress Press Books

The Vanguards of Holography - Annie Christain

Demoted Planet - Katherine Fallon

Earlier Households - Bonnie J. Morris

The Things We Bring with Us: Travel Poems - S.G. Huerta

The Water Between Us - Gillian Ebersole

Discomfort - Sarah Caulfield

The History of a Voice - Jessica Jopp

I Wish My Father - Lesléa Newman

Tender Age - Luiza Flynn-Goodlett

Low-water's Edge - Jean A. Kingsley

Routine Bloodwork - Colleen McKee

Queer Hagiographies - Audra Puchalski

Why I Never Finished My Dissertation - Laura Foley

The Princess of Pain - Carolyn Gage & Sudie Rakusin

Seed - Janice Gould

Riding with Anne Sexton - Jen Rouse

Spoiled Meat - Nicole Santalucia

Cake - Jen Rouse

The Salt and the Song - Virginia Petrucci

mad girl's crush tweet - summer jade leavitt

Saturn coming out of its Retrograde - Briana Roldan

i am this girl - gina marie bernard

Week/End - Sarah Duncan

My Girl's Green Jacket - Mary Meriam

Nuts in Nutland - Mary Meriam & Hannah Barrett

Lovely - Lesléa Newman

Teeth & Teeth - Robin Reagler

How Distant the City - Freesia McKee

Shopgirls - Marissa Higgins

Riddle - Diane Fortney

When She Woke She Was an Open Field - Hilary Brown

A Crown of Violets - Renée Vivien tr. Samantha Pious

Fireworks in the Graveyard - Joy Ladin

Social Dance - Carolyn Boll

The Force of Gratitude - Janice Gould

Spine - Sarah Caulfield

I Wore the Only Garden I've Ever Grown - Kathryn Leland

Diatribe from the Library - Farrell Greenwald Brenner

Blind Girl Grunt - Constance Merritt

Acid and Tender - Jen Rouse

Beautiful Machinery - Wendy DeGroat

Odd Mercy - Gail Thomas

The Great Scissor Hunt - Jessica K. Hylton

A Bracelet of Honeybees - Lynn Strongin

Whirlwind @ Lesbos - Risa Denenberg

The Body's Alphabet - Ann Tweedy

First name Barbie last name Doll - Maureen Bocka

Heaven to Me - Abe Louise Young

Sticky - Carter Steinmann

Tiger Laughs When You Push - Ruth Lehrer

Night Ringing - Laura Foley

Paper Cranes - Dinah Dietrich

On Loving a Saudi Girl - Carina Yun

The Burn Poems - Lynn Strongin

I Carry My Mother - Lesléa Newman

Distant Music - Joan Annsfire

The Awful Suicidal Swans - Flower Conroy

Joy Street - Laura Foley

Chiaroscuro Kisses - G.L. Morrison

The Lillian Trilogy - Mary Meriam

Lady of the Moon - Amy Lowell, Lillian Faderman, Mary Meriam

Irresistible Sonnets - ed. Mary Meriam

Lavender Review - ed. Mary Meriam

Made in the USA
Columbia, SC
09 October 2021